The CHRISTMAS FLOWER

Written by Gwen Ellis
Illustrated by Clint Hansen

Charisma KIDS

A STRANG COMPANY

The Christmas Flower
by Gwen Ellis

Requests for information may be addressed to:

The children's book imprint of Strang Communications Company
600 Rinehart Road, Lake Mary, FL 32746
www.charismakids.com

Children's Editor: Gwen Ellis
Copyeditor: Jevon Oakman Bolden
Design Director: Mark Poulalion
Designed by Bill Henderson

Library of Congress Control Number: 2004116065
International Standard Book Number: 1-59185-728-7

05 06 07 08 09 — 987654321
Printed in China

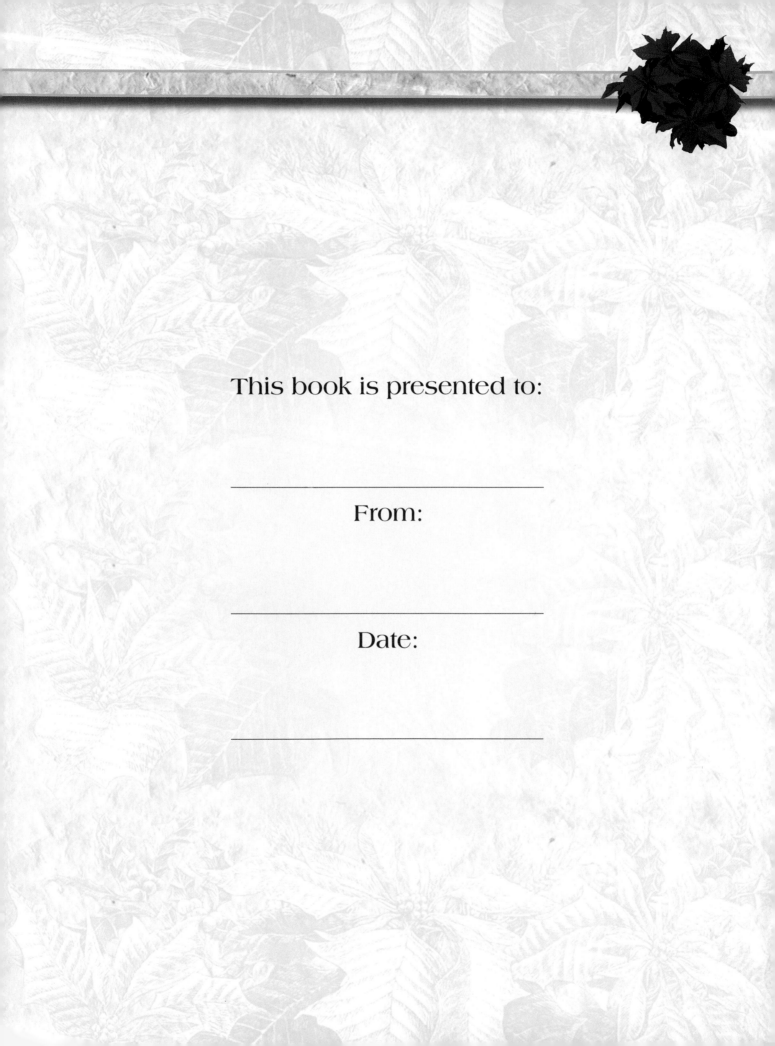

This book is presented to:

_____

From:

_____

Date:

_____

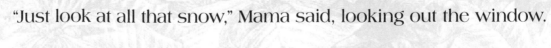
"Just look at all that snow," Mama said, looking out the window.

Sara brought a pillow and put it carefully under Mama's foot.
Mark picked up a quilt and tucked it around her.

"Does your foot hurt a lot?" Mark asked.

"It's uncomfortable," Mama sighed.

"Mama, is Daddy coming for Christmas?" Mark asked.

Mama just shook her head. "No. I wish he was though."

She looked at them. "Why don't you go look at the stores' Christmas windows? I will be fine until you get back."

Sara and Mark buttoned up their coats and went out into the bright winter sunshine.

"I wish we could buy Mama a present," said Sara.

"Me, too."

"Look!" Sara pointed to a huge red flower that almost filled the whole window of the flower shop.

"Wow!" was all Mark could say.

"That would be a wonderful present for Mama," Sara said.

"Sara, you're crazy," Mark said. "We don't have any money."

"I know, but let's ask how much it costs."

Mark rolled his eyes at his sister, but followed her into the shop.

"May I help you?" asked the flower lady.

"Yes, ma'am," Sara answered. "Can you tell us what that red flower is?"

"A poinsettia. Sometimes it's called the Christmas flower," she answered.

"Why?" Mark asked.

"Well there is a wonderful story about this flower," the lady said.
"Here, have some cinnamon cocoa, and I'll tell you the story."

She handed them the cocoa and sat down.

"Long ago in a small town, or *pueblo*, as it is called in Mexico, there were two very poor children named Pepita and Pedro."

"Poor like us," said Mark.

Sara stuck her elbow in her brother's ribs. "Shhh!"

The flower lady smiled. "It was the custom in Mexico to give a small gift to the Christ Child at Christmastime. But these poor children had nothing to give—not even a crust of bread."

"Pepita was so sad that she could hardly walk to the church with Pedro.

"'Don't be sad, Pepita,' Pedro told her. 'I'm sure you can think of something to give. Papa says there is no gift too poor for the Christ Child if you give it in love.'

"Pepita thought for a moment. Then she bent down and picked a bouquet of scraggly weeds from beside the road. This would have to be her gift. It was all she had.

"When they reached the church, Pepita hoped no one would see her weed bouquet as she crept to the manger.

"Then Pepita remembered Pedro's words. 'No gift is too poor for the Christ Child if you give it in love.' As Pepita laid her bouquet of weeds in the hay, she whispered, 'I love you, baby Jesus.'

"Instantly, the bouquet of weeds burst into bloom! All the people in the church gasped. They were sure it was a Christmas miracle.

"So they named the flowers *las flores de la Nochebuena*. That is Spanish for 'the flowers of the holy night.'"

Mark and Sara were silent. They were thinking. Then Mark said, "I wish we could buy that poin... that Christmas flower for my mama. It would make her feel better."

"What's wrong with your mother?" the flower lady asked.
Sara answered, "Mama fell on the ice and broke her foot."

"Oh," said the flower lady. She was thinking, too. "How would you like to help me until Christmas? I will pay you for the time you work, and you can buy the flowers."

"Oh, yes," Sara said. "Can we start right now?"

"Sure," she said. "Mark, please take that box out to the trash. Sara, please rewind these ribbons."

Mark and Sara worked every day after school.

At last it was Christmas Eve. "No work tonight," said the flower shop lady and gave them a hug. "This is payday. Let me wrap the poinsettia so it doesn't freeze."

The kids watched as she wrapped the paper around the plant.

Then Sara and Mark hurried home. After they stamped snow off their boots in the hallway, they burst into the living room.

"What's that?" Mama asked, smiling at them.

"A Christmas flower. And it's for you." Sara set the plant on the table.

"But...but...how?" Mama could say no more as the children removed the paper.

Then they told Mama the whole story. They told her about the flower lady, the cocoa with cinnamon, and the story of Pepita and Pedro.

"Slam!" went a car door outside. They ran to the window just as a taxi pulled away from the curb. A man with a big bag stood in the yard.

"Daddy!" yelled Mark, and he was out the door in a flash.

That evening, Sara curled up on her father's lap, and Mark scrunched up as close to him as he could get. "Daddy, how long can you stay home?" Sara asked.

"Only a few days, but I'll be home to stay very soon. What do you say we make this the best Christmas ever?"

And they did. They laughed. They sang. And Mark and Sara told their father the story of Pepita and Pedro. All through Christmas and for a long time after, the Christmas flower bloomed, reminding them that what the Christ Child wants most is our love.

The story of the Christmas flower, "The Flowers of the Holy Night" (Las Flores de la Nochebuena), is a story that has been told in Mexico for hundreds of years. What happened to the two children might be true or it might be legend. But legend or not, this story has a true and important lesson: what the Christ Child wants most is our love.

Long before Joel Robert Poinsett, U.S. ambassador to Mexico, came upon them in Taxco, Mexico, poinsettias were being cultivated by the Aztecs of Mexico. Then, because of the flowers' brilliant color and because they bloomed at Christmastime, Franciscan priests began to use poinsettias to decorate their churches for the festive season.

Mr. Poinsett was also a botanist of great ability. When he saw the plants with red flowers blooming all over the hillsides of Mexico, he sent some of them to his home in Greenville, South Carolina. There, they were carefully cultivated in greenhouses and soon Mr. Poinsett began distributing them to other growers. The popularity of the plant spread throughout the country and was given Mr. Poinsett's name. It became known as "the poinsettia"—the Christmas flower.

Help your children think of ways to show their love to Christ this Christmastime.